Cocktails with God

poems by

Heidi Elaine Hermanson

Finishing Line Press
Georgetown, Kentucky

Cocktails with God

Copyright © 2022 by Heidi Elaine Hermanson
ISBN 978-1-64662-846-9 First Edition
All rights reserved under International and Pan-American Copyright Conventions. No part of this book may be reproduced in any manner whatsoever without written permission from the publisher, except in the case of brief quotations embodied in critical articles and reviews.

ACKNOWLEDGMENTS

Many of these poems were written at Willa Cather's Second Home in Red Cloud, Nebraska, under the careful eye and direction of Laura Madeline Wiseman. Laura, I am filled with appreciation for you.

Thanks are due also to my Monday night writing group.

Thank you to Eve Donlan and Greg Kosmicki who read drafts of this and made comments.

Thanks to my family, who is always there for me.

Aaron Anstett proofread meticulously; any errors are mine.

These poems appeared, some in slightly different versions, in the following:

"Poem With A Final Line by the AAA Driver" *Plants & Poetry Journal*
"Cup Game" *Plants and Poetry Journal*
"Fool for Love" *MONO*
"St. Bridget and the Sheep" *Caesura*
"Poem With A Line By Mary Oliver" *Black Moon*
"Plastic Buddha/Hitchiking Buddha" *The Drabble*
"Raindrops—Keya Paha" *Plants and Poetry Journal*

Publisher: Leah Huete de Maines
Editor: Christen Kincaid
Cover Art: Mark Dierker
Author Photo: Al Viola
Cover Design: Heidi Elaine Hermanson

Order online: www.finishinglinepress.com
also available on amazon.com

Author inquiries and mail orders:
Finishing Line Press
PO Box 1626
Georgetown, Kentucky 40324
USA

Table of Contents

Poem with a Final Line by the AAA Truck Driver Who Fixed My Tire 1

Cup Game 2

Fool for Love 4

Voice of the Preacher 6

Saint Brigid and the Sheep 8

Too Full 9

The Bee Box 10

Weeping Willow 11

South Omaha Bridge Road 12

Spring Breakage (The Social Media Diaries) 14

Poem with a Line by Mary Oliver (Boy Fishing) 16

The Road 18

At the Wedding 19

I'll Sleep when I'm dead 20

Moonstruck 21

Twelve Views of a Silent Ignatian Retreat (Cocktails with God) ... 22

Loneliness is a Sexually Transmitted Disease 23

Plastic Buddha 24

Hitchhiking Buddha 25

Atlas 26

In Vino Veritas 27

Raindrops—Keya Paha County 28

Poem with a Final Line by the AAA Truck Driver Who Fixed My Tire

The clouds have been carefully quilted into the sky today.
The sky chooses its own shade of spectacular.
The humidity, banished to the four corners of the earth.
Trees demonstrate how easy the art of letting go is.
The lazy sun sleeps a little later every day.
I pillage hidden graveyards for bittersweet. Look here,
where the sweet bare choirs sang—
Summer has packed her bags and hit the road.

Cup Game

Pre-autumn, I wrench
the doors back from
my lazy summer when I stay
up as late as I can,
Instead, try and transform
myself to a clean and neat
8 to 5 drone.

The darkness encroaches, stealth-style,
might never disappear completely. It is a sneak
attack when the day grows shorter & shorter.
A shell game. The cup
of night comes up, masking
the cup of day. It is a cup trick.

I've made a hash
of this summer,
tubing down the Niobrara.
We all take a sigh
of relief as the
humidity leaves us
when we hit the water.

The cicadas rachet
down. Someone said cicadas
singing means only two weeks
until winter, but that
can't be right. Fall,
not spring, is a time
for new love, even
if love is falling
headfirst into a void.

The darkness spills
over the light. Squirrels
are wearing a trick
coat, not playing with
a full deck. I grow
introspective, woolgather.
Winter is inevitable.

Out on the roof, I wait
for the meteor showers.
The meteors appear
right on time, one after
another, after another.

Fool for Love

I love you like the lawnmower
loves the grass. The less
I see of you,
the better off I am.

You look beautiful but
I know about the dirt
you harbor. I loved
you like a singing bird,

happily perched. Your response
was…nothing. Can't you
hear me? Please talk
to me, I begged

you. You move
silently, before you turn
away. So—I'm mowing
my lawn, sweating

a bit, and decide the shrubs
still need trimming too. I'll need
my clippers, brand new,
hardware-store-approved

and shiny, probably in
anticipation of clipping
a few hearts.
I head to the shed.

When I open the door
I see pink ribbons
and a box of chocolate
where I usually lay the clips.

At this point I can
no longer stand it. I try
to slam the shed door shut
but apparently it's on some

kind of pneumatic device
that will not let it shut.
From behind the shed
comes a line of male

dancers nattily attired,
1920s style. They're singing
*He loves you, he loves you
not* as they pluck off

the respective petals
on the daisies! Once
again, I am caught
between a rock (the one

on my hand) and a hard
place (mostly in my mind). That's
because when someone
changes the rules capriciously

and at whim, over and over, you
have no choice but to let
your mind slip through
the cracks. It's simpler

that way. Did I tell you
I was a fool for love?

Voice of the Preacher

I do not know your name
and yet, I am the reason you exist.
It is because of me your parents
became one in soul and in flesh.
I knew when I looked
at them that this would not end well.
Something in the glint
in her eye, the trembling
of his hands. I know this was
the wrong road to drive down,
so to speak.
You perform enough
marriages, you get
a feel for these things:
broken hearts, missed
ships, broken ships,
missed chances to leave
when you should have
gotten out. I see your
Zoloft smile holding on
ever so desperately,
to what you figured
was reality—that agreed-upon
construct so many
of us took bets for, bet on,
and lost.

At a certain age
you get quiet.
It's not that you're giving
up or anything like
that—you're
conserving whatever

energy might be left
in this life. You
start thinking
more about the future,
which is another way
of saying, *The End.*

First thing you should
have done, little lady,
was get those ports (any
in a storm)
lined up. You loved
him so much (at least
in the beginning). But
you were wrong about
him; he was wrong
about you. I could
have told you so, had
you cared to listen.
But you would have
none of it—your sparkly
eyes filled
with all the possibilities inherent.
Each dish carefully arranged—cracked,
Each coffee cup, overturned.

Saint Brigid and the Sheep

Shell-shocked, sacked, shorn of all dignity
modern-day
road to escape
looked good. Beside
the ski place
the road split. Oh, you know
I took the one less traveled.
Of course I did. I thought
I was driving into hell, I drove
so far
down a narrow road that dropped
off way too sharply for comfort-
the Scottish Highlands, casket-shaped crevices
or something.
I stopped suddenly
when I saw the graveyard
on my left, and the sheep.
Sheep! All we like sheep
are stupid, seek a leader,
go astray,
and finally, meet
the knife at our throat.
Everything is a myth. Brigid
guides her sheep tenderly
as she does with everything. I put
my head out the window, yelling,
Hey sheep. Hey sheep, and when
that doesn't work, *BAAAA*.
They all turn to stare
as if I've announced
the end of the world, but
all is quiet and
goes on as usual
in their green world.

Too Full

It is in the small things
we see it. The feather
of a small brown bird,
the subtle changing
of the colors of the sky
at dawn and dusk
and before what they call
in the Midwest *weather*.
A smile from across
the room, meant only
for you. A secret.
It is the small things—
the big dog inching toward
you to be petted, his
dark eyes beseeching,
tail wagging slowly,
hitting the floor with precision
and strength.
When I arrived,
those leaves
welcomed me
as did the sky,
and the bird feather,
and the dog. This
world was too full
for me, a platter
of party appetizers,
pickles and olives
and cheese squares
waiting to be delicately
plucked up with a tiny
fork, or a toothpick with
a curl of cellophane,
as a collar on a poor
woman's party dress,
hanging in the closet
waiting to be ironed.

The Bee Box

My grandparents
practiced recycling
before 90 percent of Americans
knew what that meant.
They had a terrifying
compost heap, a grave
that emanated a dark smell
even when sealed tight shut.

Their back yard, a Garden of Eden:
apple trees
grape vines
and straight rows
of vegetables
in big boxes.
Bee hives!

Once Grandpa
put me in a bee suit,
white with a jungle hat,
netting falling like water.
I felt like a spaceman.
He assured me I was safe.
I stood,
while bees swarmed me
industriously.

In all my wanderings
I occasionally pass a bee box,
a "Hello"
from Grandpa and Grandma.

Weeping Willow

Dear Dad,
What will remind me of you most?
A stethoscope, an emerald, a prescription pad, a bottle?
You left the world at 39, not
by a .44 but a fifth.
The blue skies were not enough for you,
you had to tune them black.
Dear spell, dear drunk.
Dear cutter from the deep,
You took no effort in remaking the world—
you picked breath, heaving.
I am as sleepy as America,
eyes half-shut with her hair pinned back.
Drunkwards,
a soup of confusion,
not knowing which was soured,
a treasure chest
of medicine and whiskey.
Blank checks,
put it in your hat,
never worried about the future.
My dialect abandons the habit.
You broke all the works,
your own rules.
I am split open.

South Omaha Bridge Road

The Google HQ doesn't look like much,
A one-story building stretching
two blocks long. You'd think
it would be cheerful
multicolored swirls on the walls
—like the daily logo sometimes—
but it's beige and the few windows
have the shades drawn.
Guard box and eight stoplights,
it sits on the former site of the Council Bluffs Drive-In.
Further east, past Lake Manawa, a Target, *Bed, Bath*
("Bloodbath" my friend Barry says) *and Beyond,*
Ruth Chris' steak house, Charming Charlie,
Firehouse Subs. Programmers have to eat too.
Heading west, back to Omaha,
all manner of fancy houses with big yards
on landscaped hills, fetching bridges,
pretty much across from Malmar Acres Trailer Park.
You could fit five of your Mom's trailers
in one of these houses.
Probably the Google folks live there.
It's like some kind of Stepford-Google planned community.
The Willows motel remains yet,
a tribute to Norman Bates,
the Bottoms Up Lounge nearby.
The faded and cracked
sign reads, *"Remember to say, Bottoms Up!"*
Everything dark, as if to say
something they regretted
in another language. The South Omaha
 Bridge itself is new, crisp poured
concrete, save for the dirt gullies that gutter
into the Missouri where the Bluffs boys
 race their ATVs, so close
to the Missouri Ten years ago, Charlie wiped out,

flipped the thing over.
He hasn't walked since,
sits in his wheelchair, bums smokes,
and cheers the others on.
Do you remember?

Spring Breakage (The Social Media Diaries)

I like lying around like a reigning queen, cares,
thoughts, a tangled heap, sleep on my terms,
not the world's. I hurled
myself into my pillow, grasped

it with both arms as if it were
a long-lost friend, which was pretty
accurate if you consider it for a bit. When
I dreamt, I dreamt of unsigned

notes surreptitiously left in my mailbox,
ridiculous miniature Mexican
caballeros with empty
holsters and wicked grins.

I was quiet all week-
end. I built a moat of pink
and yellow dots all around
my bed. They kept the dragons

floating below at bay,
but they also kept me
in the bed. He had told me, kindly
and tactfully, that I made a good

friend. He didn't tell me in person
what he'd splashed all over his
Facebook—his new and improved
"relationship status." She

was very blonde and very thin
and had a PhD
in relationships. The same placid
non-expression on my face,

a mask, a book that only
I could read. If anyone were
to ask, I was fine. I would say:
My heart beats clear

and regular. My eyes
close of themselves
at night. My breathing
is light and even,
asleep or awake. I am
sure this meant very little to him.

Poem with a line by Mary Oliver (Boy Fishing)

It is in a small
drop of rain that
everything is magnified.

A sky crammed with clouds
racing along.

A still pond interrupted
by one splash
of fish.

A boy fishing,
intent, this moment
his whole world.
He has a dog-eared
book beside him.
He is poring
over the words:

*In the book
of the earth it is written,
nothing can die.*
He likes the way
the cover depicts
the author:
grim and ancient.

He yawns. It has been a long
strenuous day, searching
for carp. So few of them.
The sun is ticking slowly
across the sky—so slow
it is nearly unnoticeable until
suddenly, evening
and he must pick

up his fishing gear
and his lunch pail

and go down the long,
lean, dirt path,
surrounded by the blue
and pink twilight,
the blue cover
and further up,
the stars.

The Road

The road is calling
me again, that old bum. He
knows how I love
an unshaven face. There

must be something
beautiful waiting for me
down that dusty road. Some
fine lake surrounded

by grape trellises. An abandoned
house, its joints creaking
with age and wind, eyes of windows
gaping at the sight

of the first visitor in
forty years. Just behind
the house, a graveyard filled
with stones ancient and crumbling, words
erased out by time, weeds and flowers gone

wild. A pink rose bush releases
its scent. There was a road
to it once, but it's grown
over, blocked by time and memories.

At the Wedding

Kaytee,

Pixie,
you washed into our lives
like a drunken mermaid, joyous and singing.

Joan of Arc brave,
ardent light bearer, paladin,
you never hesitate to set the world right,
or possibly, on fire.

You wield panache, and sass,
 kindness honed to the sharpest blade.
You flit, extract and scatter joy like rose petals on the wind.

And now you have met him, the beloved,
the one who flutters
your radiant heart, who tends your tenderness,
The one you will love forever, a canvas
to paint on together.

Your heart, ceded, glows like rose quartz,
durable and solid, expansive and gleaming
as you open your book of questions addressed to each hour,
braiding each moment
as you face the sunrise, its splendid
cadence of light bittersweet,
your cornflower eyes clear
as a river
as you and he
make the world new
over and over again.

I'll Sleep When I'm Dead
(near Crab Orchard, Nebraska)

Nothing lasts forever
not wind
not rain
not sorrow
in the bright sun
and cool breeze
in these acres of wild roses.
Lying down, hand to the sun,
to nap,
perhaps to dream,
under golden tendrils of time
long gone,
filigree framing the sky
and windmills, the only angels.

Moonstruck

A small Iowa town with beautiful
lights like a Cheshire
palace, or a space
ship. I will not say velvety
night. I will say dust-covered,
tired, glowing skies,
a stream of pink
then fade to blue,
and then darkest blue.
You smell green,
the green of summer
that lingers long
after summer. You smell
gasoline, you smell
corn silk. Your pulse
quickens, for how often
do you hear gospel music
out here on the plains, out
here on the interstate?
The music fades and the moon
slowly rises, huge and ruddy
and as full as you have ever
seen it, a plum to be picked,
an orange to be picked? No,
none of these will do. You think
you should believe in life
on other planets, you think
it is all true and anything
is possible. She smiles
coyly, a face you never
tire of seeing, a penny
you can spend over and over again.

Twelve Views of a Silent Ignatian Retreat (Cocktails with God)

1. The trails are muddy. We could walk down them, but we had to walk back up. We were warned.

2. Last night I started to have a hypnogogic sleep state, and said out loud, "Now, don't freak out," and went straightaway back to sleep. I think there is great power in this place.

3. But is there a map?

4. One woman couldn't talk so she danced. Danced in front of the oatmeal dish—performed an "I don't know" with her shoulders.

5. A nod and a smile works as well as a thank you when your tongue is locked up.

6. For some, silent means talking in another room (*If no one can hear me, I must not be talking*), or talking in a whisper (*Whispering isn't talking*). For others, it's sign language. Or notes.

7. "We are people of poor memory and limited perspective." –Father John

8. The pen, oh, the clicking pen…

9. Every day here feels like Sunday, bright and unfilled.

10. "It's always about being on the way." –Father John

11. Potter, clay—my life splattered all over God.

12. "There is nowhere else to go." –Father John

Loneliness is a Sexually Transmitted Disease

Caution!
Be sure to practice
all the good hygiene
after the big breakup:
Viruses are infectious.
While you're up late
tying knots in love's thread,
take a long hot breath
and soak what hurts most
in Epsom salts and water. Pour
chocolate syrup
on your toast. Crying
may jump-start your healing;
Moscato calms the heart.
There is no pill for loneliness.

Plastic Buddha

I want a plastic Buddha—
I'll put him on my dashboard
and fly away.
We'll eat shitty snacks
and laugh about that
"body of a god" joke
before drowsing in the summer heat
under the Bodhi Tree.

Hitchhiking Buddha

The Buddha was riding in my car
He was fifteen feet tall
and looked more like Chuck Norris
than the gloss of Christ. He
had spread out ham, beef, tortillas,
and PBR
(come and eat and
drink without price and
without money)
like that verse in Psalms.
Later, he said,
Let's find a nice watering
hole and go swimming.

Atlas

Your life, a road
trip with no destination
and no itinerary, unfolds
slowly like a crumpled
roadmap. The blue
lines glow and you feel
yourself drawn into
it—rivers, lakes,
roads become real. You
float peacefully over
the landscape, like
being on the inside
of a cathedral. You finally
have that time to yourself.
The sickly-sweet aroma
of incense. Your life.

In Vino Veritas

Can I enter a room filled
with beautiful people

and be at ease; do I pass
for sane?

Splash of wine,
laughter. Smoke rises,

an offering, as confessions
are made, deals are sealed,

confidences betrayed.
But my hands and feet

are two sizes larger
since we came in.

Still I laugh and nod my head.
I smile wisely.

The artist Kay Sage once
said, "I live in a world

where the only truth
is dreaming." Well then,

if all I have is a dream,
I shall dream. Pour the wine

and sit down. We have bread
to break, stories to relate.

Let the night go where
it will, moon so lonely,

stars huddled together
for warmth.

Raindrops—Keya Paha County, Nebraska

The angels were silent that day,
while the moon stalked me like an old lover.
He told me if we can fuse laughter and tears we are doing the work.

She's light years ahead of everyone. She carries a light
saber and writes in great swathes on their hearts.
If you are disappointed, I am not sorry.

I was telling the story, but people
kept talking—it got too complicated, so I stopped.
I suppose that dumb crumb is supposed to satisfy me.

The palm of her hand:
the poem of her hand.
The sign read: *Protecting today's perishables for tomorrow.*

My idea of speed is 40 miles an hour breakneck down a
gravel road dust tall weeds trees—cows agape.
Fifties in the elevator, nineties in the foyer.

Raindrops stop me cold: The old descent holds me for a moment,
then lets me spin.
Missed Connections: Me asking about gilts. You: Handsome
country vet, devastating blue eyes.
No one needed anything, anymore.

Heidi Hermanson is a first-generation Nebraskan who has been published in *Midwest Quarterly, Hiram Poetry Review, the Omaha World Herald* ("Nebraska On A Dollar a Day") and elsewhere. She has been in public art projects such as "8 counts/24" (writers had 24 hours to write on a theme pulled randomly from a hat) and the benchMarks project, which featured brief inspirational quotes on bus benches throughout the city. She organized the first Poets' Chautauqua at the State Fair and there released her first chapbook, *Midwest Hotel*. The recipient of two Pushcart nominations, a Nebraska book award, and various grants from both Amplify Arts and The Nebraska Arts Council, Heidi has organized and directed five ekphrastic shows which she describes as a marriage between visual art and poetry. From 2006 to 2012 she ran "Naked Words", a monthly open mike. In 2010 she won the Omaha Public Library's annual poetry contest and performed her winning work accompanied by Silver Roots, a New York-based violin and flute duo. She has read at the John R Milton Conference in Vermillion, SD, at the Bowery Poetry Club in New York City, at Tunes in the Town Square (which features poetry at the band's break) in Ralston, Nebraska, on the Kerry Pedestrian Bridge over the Missouri, and at the Roebuck Pub in England. In her spare time she hopes to open a library of maps to towns that do not exist and learn the dialects of the seven-year cicada. In 2008 Heidi received her MFA from the University of Nebraska at Omaha and released her first book, *Waking to the Dream* in 2018. Having found herself with an abundance of time during the pandemic, she enjoys exploring every square foot of her state and documenting cemeteries and rivers.

www.ingramcontent.com/pod-product-compliance
Lightning Source LLC
LaVergne TN
LVHW041515070426
835507LV00012B/1590